AF596188

Destiny

Select Poems

Sarah McHatton

For information contact:
Sarah McHatton
smchatton.writer@gmail.com

ISBN: 9798351596693
Imprint: Independently published

First Published September 2022

Sometimes life takes us in a direction we don't understand. It is our job to hold on and enjoy the ride.

Acknowledgements

Emma Deaton – You have been such a help to me in the last few months. Know that space may be between us, but our friendship will never change. I love you and miss you greatly!

Denise Smith – You amaze me every day with your drive. Keep it up!

Julio Gil – I cannot find the words to thank you for your support, your trust in us, and your love. You mean the world to us. Without you, we wouldn't be here and so secure.

Reid – Thanks for the friendship! And all the memes!

To the Reader

Life certainly has a way of changing the path you walk on without much choice. The poems inside this book are a reflection of memories and an exploration of the connection of memory, life, and nature. I have been inspired by certain celestial art pieces that spark my imagination. I allowed the words to flow and my mind to wander leading to some amazing work. Thanks for coming along on the journey.

Sarah McHatton

A Grief So Deep

The tears came

Unsure and unabashed

Exposing my grief

To those closest to me

I longed to hide

Keeping my vulnerability

Closer to my heart

Without acknowledging

How misty mountains

Could imbed themselves

So deeply in my soul

How leaving them

Felt like I was tearing

A piece of my soul

From my chest

Leaving it to float

Along with the ghosts

Of my ancestors

Of my mother

In those misty mouns'

I try to smile

Hide the pain and fear

To ease the suffering

Of those I care about

Knowing I called this change

Longing for a release

From trauma filled memories

And years of torment

At the hands of those

Who share my blood

I try to take solace

In future new experiences

Taking one day at a time

And hoping, that hole

Finds a way to fill

A moment or a memory

A future or a hope

To change the direction

I know, deep within my soul

I will carry the grief

Of what I left behind

Each step I take, each day

Each minute and each second

Until those misty mountains

Filling my gaze once more

A Kiss

A kiss so delicate

Was placed

On the tip of my nose

As I look

Into your chocolate eyes

The air in my lungs

Puffed out in chilly bursts

Chasing the Cheshire moon

Aglow

Mist hung in the air

Heavy like a bated breath

As she took a deep sigh

Her hand reached out for

The umbrella, clear and open

Holding it over her head

Blocking the wetness

From her auburn hair

Stopping the chance for

A shoulder length frizzy mess

The moon hung lively

Cheshire smiling to all who saw

As she walked, step-by-step

Through the dewy field

Stars blazed into the air

Passing by her, crashing

Into the moist earth

Leaving shards of stardust

Her steps fell between

Golden, sparkling stars

Departed their heavenly roost

The sky alight with more

Matched by the earth

Finding a new bind

    Lost in time

    Aglow with potential

All the Things

All the things I should have said

All the hugs I should have gave

All the tears I should have wiped away

All the pain I should have taken

When you brought me to this world

I was weak and small

You gave me strength

And helped me to grow

You gave me life

And kissed my pains away

Gave me hugs every day

Your hands held me tight

And wiped away my tears of fright

You kissed my cheek

And whispered comforts in my ear

Now it's too late to tell you

How you changed my life

How you taught me to be

The best I could be

You left my life too early

And left me with memories

And now it's too late

To tell you that I love you

All that is left is sadness

The pain that helps it grow

I have but one small dream

That's to have you back with me

Why did you have to go

And leave me here to deal

With this unending grief

You said you loved me

With all your heart

Now you are in someone else's arms

All the things I should have said

All the love I hid from you

All the words that didn't come out right

All the pain left inside

All the tears that didn't fall

All the thoughts we didn't share

All the time wasted

Now I am left, without you

I try to move on

To live my life without you

But my heart is shattered

Into pieces I try to mend

But I am without

The strength to go on

Any Day

Any day, I'll be there

Any way I can

I'm going to get there

And you're going to be my man

You're going to love me right

You're going to hug me tight

You're going to kiss my soft lips

And tug at my hips

Your love is a need

Of mine all along

Beaten

A kind word unspoken

World full of judgment

Lives shortened and uncaring

For those who need comfort

My heart aches at the ignorance

The insolence and the lack of compassion

For our fellow human beings

So different, yet so similar

How would we feel, in their situation?

Starved, disable, and unable to work?

Struggling, wounded, and destroyed

Chewed up and spit out, unwanted.

Can you truly take a step

A step in someone's life

If that person struggles

And strains each day

Do we judge someone's merits

Or the content of their hearts

On something unchanging

Like skin tone, disability or birth

Life is full of judgment and injustice

Yet, when those are turned toward us

We cry and complain, with voices raised high

Without a care of fellow humans

It becomes easier to turn a blind eye

Toward the plight of others

Instead of showing integrity, compassion, and love

For a person crying for help

We seek the parallel life

Where the life we want

Is the one we live

Yet, at what cost?

The cost of lives, hunger and struggle

The dying earth, gasping for breath

Greed around every corner

Death, murder, mayhem and plague

What will it take to turn an eye

Toward the corruption of man

In the world that covets

The reasons we become corrupt

Youth allowed blinders to the world

As youth is stripped away

Those blinders disappear, providing

An unchanged view of man

Thousands of years of greed

Murdering, war for power

For land, for resources

Until conquering becomes paramount

Where civilizations, thousands of years old

Were murdered, plagued and docile

Too weak to fight, too beaten to defeat

A land that belonged to them

Before

My heart aches. Tears fall from my eyes

Wishing you were here with me

Holding me in your arms

Looking into my eyes, and kissing my lips softly

Less than 24 hours, my wishes will come true

My hopes are that you love me

No matter what and that you always will

My biggest fear is that you won't

A fear that haunts me all the time

One which never goes away

Well maybe in time

But not any time soon

I hope you don't know how

To quiet something you do well

And hope you realize that life is short

To let this love pass you by

Time will soon tell if our love is true

And if we can continue what we have

Although it's for such a short time

We will enjoy every moment we share

Come On Baby

Snow is falling

The seasons calling

So bright and lively

As the days go by

Just one thing is missing

As the season glistens

It would be so perfect

If you were mine

Come share a blanket

With me, you can just see

How perfect we can be

Together as one

Make my season

Just a breezin'

Give me the present I want

Come on baby

Don't mistake me

Give me your heart

The most precious present

You know you want me

Just to be yours

Come on baby

Let's make a start

Death of a Flower

The petal curls lightly

As it opens to death

Color draining

A small life away

Taking its everlasting

Breath

And turning the minutes

Into a day

The first petal falls

Softly through the air

Dropping gently

As each follows

Floating down

Greeting death

With a colorful flutter

Desperate

Desperate

For love

Desperate to see

To be seen

As who I am

Who I am truly

Without a guise to hide

Drawn

Underneath the sultry summer sky

Filled with fluffy white clouds

I sat, face tilted up

Taking in the rays of sun

Feeling the warmth on my face

Until movement brought my eyes

To an older woman

Walking at a fast clip

Across the pavement

Her face, etched with pain

Sorrow filled the spaces

And created thick lines

Hardened by years of toil

I watched, enthralled

Pulled towards her

Unable to turn my gaze away

As if something drew my attention

Some deeper meaning

I could almost feel her pain

The harshness of her breath

Aching my lungs

The clomp of her feet

Jarring through my soles

The tension of her shoulders

Pulling at my neck

I watched until she turned

Around the corner

And out of view forever

Wondering why I felt drawn

To the plight of someone

Unknown to me

Expanse

I am falling, faster and faster

Through the endless expanse of night

The stars are blurry, streaks of light

Like tinsel hanging in the darkness

Illuminated with luminosity

Filling my eyes with twinkles

So in awe, fear disappears

Leaving me with a sense of wonder

The air thickens, slowing my fall

I see the stars shorten

Popping into existence around me

I risk a look below me

Seeing a flat expanse of reflection

Showcasing the twinkling stars

My mouth opens to a perfect "Oh"

Lost in the majesty of the galaxy

The crescent moon cradles me

Until I sit, perched on the edge

My toes submerge into warm wetness

Creating ripples in the reflection

Morphing the stars into a fake image

Until the water settles

I sigh, feeling peace drift

Taking over the reins

The tension in my body escapes

Leaving me slumped, seated

Hands tucked under my thighs

I peer into the reflection

Silence, stillness surrounds me

Lost in this moment

With nothing but myself

And the expanse of stars

Perfectly reflected below my feet

Everything I am, everything I was

Everything I will be doesn't matter

My breath slows and I close my eyes

To the brilliance of time

Part of me knows I should feel lonely

Lost on the sea and yet, I feel peace

Seeing the potential, knowing the truth

In the distance, a star brightens

Blinking brilliant and strong

Then disappears with a pop

I am transfixed to that spot

As the light fades away

More stars ping to life

Filling the space once overflowing

With the chance, with life

With overwhelming possibility

In that moment, the realization

That something had to die,

Had to disappear, for other opportunities

For memories, for hopes and dreams

For futures, for time, for life

To grow and be seen

To flicker into existence

And bring with it abundance

I shift, laying down

Cradled in the crescent moon

Letting my hand trail in the water

As my eyes fill with stars

And my soul fill with hopes and dreams

Against the endless expanse

Of possibilities and futures

Exposed

All of me, my heart, my thoughts

I give them to you on paper

Words ripped from my very soul

Spliced onto thinned and dry pulp

Words I dare not speak aloud

Words that expose me, all of me

My very weaknesses before you

To expose and use, shards

As if my soul shatters

Placing fragile pieces at your feet

A gasp rips from me

Until I am left shaking

Tears flowing down my cheeks

Knowing, at last, the words

That ached to come out

Have covered the pages

Strength they tell me

Vulnerability is a strength

But I find it hard

Very hard indeed to believe

Flood

The rain doesn't seem to slacken

Causing worry and concern

In the dark, she stands

Shadow casting deep and long

The roar of the water, a few feet away

Is deafening to her ears

As it bobs and sways

Over anything standing in its way

The sight is amazingly breathtaking

Even as fear walks down her spine

One wrong movement on her part

Means a fall and a drowning

The power of rushing water

Is amazing and oh so scary

For when she looks in the muddy depths

She sees death's reflection

Dirt and debris flow

Just the same

Carrying down the river

Floating without blame

Her body tenses, head to toe

As a gust of wind blows

Knocking against her

With frightening strength

What a way to end a life

Swept away by the forces of nature

As she stands and stares

Her body shivers

Turning away she smiles

For she has seen power

Rising in the deep, seducing

And she won

As she walks away

The sun comes out with a bow

Frayed

Overwhelmed and lost

The grief of a life I had

Memories fill the walls

Echoing like a voice

Against the distant mountains

Replete with emotions

Some good, some bad

Here I am, perched on the edge

Of an important decision

Washing the walls of my home

Scrubbing away dust and debris

As thoughts cascade

Through my exhausted mind

I am afraid of the future

And for the future

Uncertain, not for the first time

But lost in the chaos

That surrounds me in this moment

Housing crisis, depression, recession

Buzz words echoing on the screen

In news stories, and unfortunately

Out of the mouths of property managers

As we seek a new place

A new home, a future

I feel lost, unable to give much comfort

To those I love as they stare

Into the same abyss, hand-in-hand

Three worlds, three people

Perched on the same cliff

With no net, no hope

As each no echoes

Across phones and in our face

Each draining day

Sapping more energy

From my withering soul

And the hope for a better future

The mountain strong

Echoing in my veins

Assures me I will survive

Thousands of years

Of human existence

Of striving and thriving

Assures me I should be fine

Etched with pain and torment

Deep struggle and hard work

And still, my soul trembles

At a life, a comfy enough life

That is now passed me by

The wanderlust has grown

Deep within my soul

Slowly etching a path

I wish I could take

Is this the moment

Where my feet start walking

Is this the moment

I accept uncertainty

For what it is

And not a fear best avoided

To take a little step

Toward a moment, a simple moment

Where I choose me and the future

Not a moment where I am stuck

Stuck in a horrific set of moments

Nightmares of my past

Flaying me alive, bleeding me

Until I lay wounded

And barely conscious on the ground

I have no clue how to be

Both of those people

The woman who can move mountains

For her family, stressed and stretched

Thin and rugged by years of hard work

And the broken woman

Torn apart by the memory of hands

Of harsh words and moments

Ripped apart by someone else's

Selfish and fool-hardy behavior

I know, deep down, I am that woman

Both those women, forged together

By years of furious hand stitching

Bloodied and beaten, reaching for

The thread that keeps it all together

I try to find the peace

In knowing that is all I need to do

Keep threading, keep pulling

The fabric of my life together

And whip stitching frayed fabric

But it brings me no peace

So here I sit, lost and feeling alone

Hand-in-hand with two

Perched on the edge of a cliff

Hoping the fabric of my life

Is stitched enough

To parachute us to something better

Leaving us whole, together

Instead of ripped to shreds

Lost to our own cruel world

How Do I Choose

Change is coming

Going to rock my world

Left me to decide

Plagued with pain

And anger washing over me

How do I choose

A time or a place

To explain, to decide

To react, how do I choose

Sick to my stomach

Tension building in my shoulder

Screaming anguish, wracking

My body and my mind

I Feel so Free

I want you to know

How much you mean to me

Oh how life used to be

I feel so free, I can breathe

You are a breath of fresh air

In a world of staleness

Oh how life used to be

Thank you, I feel so free

Life left me down and out

Without a hope

I didn't think I could come out

Barely able to breathe

With everything choking me

And you were there

Holding out a hand

Thank you, I feel so free

The time grew grey

Without you here

You left me there

No pain, no grief

Time when by

But you're words

Still get me

I barely get by

But I don't worry

I don't fault you

For once I stand alone

Thank you, I feel so free

I Hope

I hope I never steer you away

My love grows stronger every day

Time can never tell you

Where you went wrong

The promises you gave me

Handed me a greater love of life

You showed me a world

I have never known

And pushed me to be better

Than I have ever been

You had faith in me

When I had none in myself

And supported me

Through everything in life

The faith I have

You gave to me

The fears I dream

Are kissed away

By your lips,

My soul is soothed

Thank you

My dear

I Promise

I promise to you

That I will always love you

For who you are

And the wonderful man

You will become

I promise to never allow

What you do or what you don't do

To interfere with any of the love

I have for you

And with you

I promise to be by your side

When you want me to be

No matter the time, the place

No matter what has happened

Or what will

I promise to be your best listener

Whether it is to vent frustrations

To share your dreams

Or to just chat about the weather

Anything, light or dark

I promise to share my thoughts

My feelings, deep and unseeded

Even if it hurts

Despite the pain, sorrow

Despite the grief

I promise to share every event

Every moment of your life

That you believe to be worthy

Of being a memory of yours

Of mine, and of ours

I promise to trust you

In all that you do

What you say

What you do

Every moment

I promise to be honest

As open as I can

Despite any test

Placed in our path

In the years to come

I promise to never hold

The past against you

No matter the conflict

For it builds walls

That we cannot take away

I promise to be open

As I hope you will be

When I feel strongly

On a topic I may blow

Out of proportion

I promise to support you

In the decisions you make

Plan or unplanned

Together we will always

Stand hand-in-hand

I promise to keep you sane
Despite the outside world
Pushing and pulling
Crushing you under the weight
I will be there

I promise to be your haven
A place of sanctuary
To hide, to curl up to
A shelter always and forever
When you need to slip away

I promise to stay
Perched by your side
Walking step-by-step
Beside you, with you, for you
Come what may

I Wonder

I wonder if you see me

As you

What I wouldn't give

For a glance or look

My way

Icicles

Drips of water, trapped

In a cylindrical shape

Sharp and clear

Sparkling and shimmering

When the sun hits them

Bright against the white snow

Lapping

I long to sit along the seaside

Eyes closed, body drawn

Arms around my knees

Simply listening

Hearing the sounds of the surf

Lapping at my feet

As the tide rises

The waves crashing against sand

Underneath the canopy

Of brightly, flickering stars

Like fireflies against the trees

Deep in summer in the Smokies

I long to feel the wind

Caressing the bare skin of my neck

Pushing and lifting my hair

Teasing the tiny hairs

Into a feeling of aliveness

Exposing me to a world

A world beyond myself

I long to open my eyes

To stare out into the dark abyss

Without fear, without worry

Knowing that the horizon

I cannot see in this moment

Still lies out of reach

Hidden by the darkness

Of the depths of night

I long, I long

For the sparkles of bioluminescent

Twinkling in the surf

Caressing me, surrounding me

As the surf twists and pulls

Ebbs and wanes

Beneath the star filled sky

Instead I sit

Perched in indecision,

Uncertainty

Longing for hope

For a dream

And for the peace

That comes with

A certain future

Like a Dream

Life seems like a dream

Filled with joy

Happiness, love and hate

It slips away slowly

And then leaves quickly

Death comes unexpected

Sometimes early

Sometimes late

Death makes the joy leave

Replacing it with grief

Little Regard

You said no
While my feet were
Two sizes above
What they should be
Swollen from standing
Too long, no rest
While my back ached
With every movement
Hurt with every stretch
I watched her
Getting the short end
Of every stick
Even on her deathbed
Watched as she was used
For the last dollars
In her purse
Chosen last after a job

After drugs

After alcohol

After your own lives

In the quietness

She knew

That the life of a mother

Held little regard

For her own wellbeing

For her own wants

And until this moment

I failed to realize

That her choice of love

Was her own selfishness

Her own desires come

To the life she wanted

She and I will forever

Be tied to the end

Of her life

Both longing for relief

Each suffering loss

Love

Feel the grasp

Of our being

Each other

As life

Is so short

Memories

It's a sight, a sound

A moment when life comes back

A memory lost, waiting to be found

It is those moments I relish

Bear cubs, chocolate chip cookie dough ice cream

Basketball, Arby's, Fireworks, camping

Kittens, s'mores, eggs and lake

Each and everything that helped shape

A kind word, a new parent

A baby born, crying into the world

The rattle of a train on tracks

The sweet smell of cows and pasture

Frogs croaking in the night

As fireflies light up the sky

The wind against my face

As I sail on my bike

The rustling of grass

The heavy, cool rains

That beat against my skin

A moment when memories come back

Missed

I miss the way you put your arms around me

And the way you touch my soft skin

I miss the way you play with my hair

And the way you kiss my neck

I miss the way you look at me

And the way you bend to kiss my lips

I miss the way you pull me close

And the way you hold me tight

I miss the whispers in my ear

And the way you nibble and kiss my breasts

I miss the way you gaze at me

And the way you lick your lips

I miss the way you smile as you laugh

And the way you tickle me lightly

I miss the way your stubble tickles me

And the way you kiss my forehead

I miss the way you shared with me

And the way you breathe

I miss the way you sleep

And the way you watch me when you wake

I miss watching you as you sleep

And looking into your eyes

I miss reaching up to kiss you

And hugging you tight

My Prison

I sit, perched in a cage

With the key within my reach

Everything I try

Never brings me closer

To the key to my freedom

Lost, searching aimlessly

For a life I didn't live

Preyed upon by my demons

Forever haunting me

I open myself

Despite the years of pain

Knowing rejections, ridicule

Heartache and sorrow come

Undoubtedly as sure as the sun rises

And still, I reach

Pressing my face against the bars

Seeking release

From the bars that bind me

The demons that flay me

And the memories

    The memories that never

    EVER float away

Oh

Oh how I miss your wonderful smile

And how you look at me deeply

I can't wait until the day

You hold me in your strong warm arms

You can never know how bad I miss you

And how bad I want to be with you

On the Moon

I saw them falling

So I rushed out

To greet them

Bright and golden

I stood, as they dropped

Into the cooling earth

Around my warm body

Pulsing with energy

My hand reaches

Out to caress

The trail of sparkles

They left in the air

I smile, watching

The gold dust fly

Animated, joyous

In the still air

A part of me

Feels desperate

With need and longing

To fix the quandary

That I saw before me

One where these stars

Have a deep hold

In the heavens above

A ladder, my mind screams

Sure it could extend to

The Cheshire moon

Hazy blue and smiling

I run across the grass

Through swirling luster

To the old wooden barn

Seized, I wobble forward

Searching for the right spot

To place, precariously

This wooden ladder

A ladder I hope

Will spring to life

Golden dust swirls

Wrapping around

Latching onto the wood

Coating it with vigor

I watch as the ladder

Stretches forth

Creating rungs quickly

Reaching out in speed

Without haste, I grab a handful

Sure I can carry more

And take the rungs

One at a time

Holding on with one hand

I climb and climb

Until the earth disappears

Leaving me high

High in the night sky

Surrounded by the light

Brilliant and effervescent

In this space, I feel alone

With only the stars

And the Cheshire moon

To keep me company

Climbing, I keep climbing

Until the chill freezes

My breath out in spurts

Of icy goodness

Until I stand, barefoot

On the smile of the moon

I tiptoe forward

Smiling as I go

Until my toes, wiggling so

Touches the edge

Holding the rest in one arm

I hold a star, golden

Lifting my hand, I reach

Letting the star rise

Shivering with anticipation

Floating into the sky

Back into the expanse

Floating before me

I smile, as I reach for another

Sure they will be safe

    Hold up in the sky

    Safe to fall another day

On Top of the World

You have given me

A love like no other could give

You have made me so happy

I am on top of the world

You have shared with me

A life we both wish was unlived

You make me smile like any other

I am on top of the world

You have given me comfort

Something I could hardly find

You have opened your arms to me

I am on top of the world

You have made my life complete

With every word, phrase, and action

You showed me how to love

I am on top of the world

You have given me everything I wanted

A man who loves me for everything

I can give and who I am

I am on top of the world

You are my love, my everything

I want to thank you

From the bottom of my heart

I am on top of the world.

Path

Time withstanding

Across a brilliant wood

Vines intertwined

Cascading around me

As I stand

Back against the world

My heart stops

At the view

Clutched between peace

And chaos

My breast warms

In the glow

As my back freezes

In icy grip of chaos

Perched, walking the fine line

Until I choose

A life of simplicity

Or one of materialism

Structure or freedom

Pain or pleasure

A hard choice

To walk among the many

Or walk among the few

Do I concede to the voices

Raised before me

Whispering along the road

The road not taken

Do I sway under the pressure

Or do I step into the unknown

To allow my footsteps

To create a new path

One where whispers

Remain unheard

A path overgrown

Until many feet tread

Do I concede to a life

Chosen for me

Or do I follow

This ever beating heart

Poised inside my chest

To choose a life of my own

Free from judgment

Free from prejudices

Can I choose to let my voice

Be raised above all others

To be heard

By swayable ears

Can I choose to dance

Under the harvest moon

A life once controlled

A voice once quieted

A worth hidden

Now, chosen, treasured

Raised on a path

The path less taken

Root

A cascade of emotions

Echoes in my veins

Like the song of the katydid

Through the lanes

Underneath a night sky

Filled with moonlight

I stand taking it all in

Deep inside, feeling a fright

Wondering if I will see

These same mountains again

Creek to creek, trees abound

Into the rocky glen

My ancestors, born of nature

Crafted strong by hardship and time

Endured the same treatment

Forced to do the walk and climb

I feel a shiver

Slip down my body

All I wanted to accomplish

Is be somebody

Instead, I stand here

Below the harvest moon

Laid bare, broken

All my emotions strewn

Onto the wet grass

Under a silvery cloud

Waiting for the moon

To disappear and enshroud

Wishing for that moment

For time, for my hopes

To root like oaks

Roots

A plea, a hope

A prayer, a thought

Hidden, but spoken

Beneath the surface

A grand emotion

Shard

The pain endured

During the best years

Of a life was hard

Tearing at everything

Inside like flesh

With a crystal shard

Share Love

How can I ever share

The love you have given me

A love so great

That no word could explain

You have given me

Your world, your life, your love

Without expecting much

Beyond the same in return

A love so great and willing

When you asked me

To be yours forever

All time stopped

Leaving us in our world

Never had I imagined

I would share a life

With you, for you

Someone who loves me

Someone who cares

Share

Watch the sky

Lightening, dark against

The tall mountain peaks

Hear the songs

Of the birds in the trees

Speak the words

Found within my heart

For as the day lengthens

And time slows to a stop

We are reminded

To share our love

With those we love

And soon will lose

Short

How do I choose

Who makes me happy

How do I choose

The love of my life

Smiles

In the pale moon, I wish I saw

Her face once again smiling at me

But isn't that natural law

To want and be carefree

Living in a world that makes sense

Being able to be open and vulnerable

Without having to put up a defense

To be more accountable

To those who love us and who we love

Without fear of reprisal

Someone to be proud of

But her smile, oh what an eyeful

My mother brought light

Into this bleak and lonely world

Seeking love and joy as a right

Almost as if love twirled

She tried her hardest

To love and be loved

Sometimes to be honest

When life shoved and she felt unloved

The most unfortunate thing

Is to know there were moments

That she had a downswing

And faced no acknowledgments

For the woman she was

And the flaws she held

For a man, all because

His anger couldn't be quelled

She was kept at arm's length

Taking time away from us

All on the same wave length

Man, it feels so treasonous

For the little girl in me

Still trying to understand

What caused her to flee

I want to know firsthand

So I am left unknowing

The memories and the trials

Of the woman, forgoing

All I wish for is the smiles

Spiraling

I felt the fear rising

Deep beneath my chest bone

Panic careening through

Every fiber of my body

How could I keep my family

Together and sane

Through this craziness

Is it possible? Is this real?

Weeks of panicked looking

Searching for a home

Footstep upon footstep

To be greeted with a no

All the hope for the future

Met with resounding denial

With tears and frustrations

Sitting in a chair, encased

In a profound twilight

Alone and crying

No hope for a future

Unsure and unsettled

Homelessness arriving

Faster than I wanted to admit

I stood, resolute

In whatever came in the future

I reached for a box

Placing tape across the edges

Cinching them together

Slowly, I place our life

Piece by piece into storage

Day by day, moment by moment

Until we leave forging a new life

In a much bigger city

Uncomfortable with the uncertainty

That hovers over us like a haint

I feel overwhelmed

Knowing that I, in my thirty-eight years

Lived with more stability and security

I cared to acknowledge

Always aware that I had a safety net

And now, it doesn't exist

We float, unsecure and unstable

In the winds of change

Hoping for the day our feet

Plant firmly on the ground

Able and willing to have stability

A home, a life, a future

Sunlight

Chilled dirt falls carelessly through her fingers

As she scoops a handful to the side

Ever so gently, she places the bulb

Into the chilly earth for it to rise

Awakened rough the power of sun

To break through the crust of organic material

And reaching out, leaves stretched to touch the sky

Her creator, her savior

Pulling her to her embrace

Thank You

Thank you for loving me

For all I am and can be

Thank you for caring

So much for me

Thank you for being there

To wipe away my tears

And to take away my fears

Thank you for holding me

In your loving arms

In which comes, no harm

Thank you for trusting me

Like you do

And making me laugh

When I am blue

The Christmas Kiss

Mistletoe hangs above our heads

The fire crackles in the fire place

There's love all around

To spice up the holiday

But you're here

And that's all that matters

Year after year

Christmas comes and goes

As the snow falls

To the ground

We lean in for a kiss

And the bells chime

Echoing across the mountains

And peace reigns

Deep inside

I lean my head down

On your shoulder

As we gaze out

Into the snowy evening

The mole pranced down the burrow

Calling to the three, sitting together

The Night Sky

The notes hid themselves

Among the surf, careening

Across the wet sand

With each push of the waves

A rush of water, spraying mist

And the retreat, silent

The plaintive notes of a piano

Filling the air, haunting

Pulling his soul like a siren

Calling him to the seaside

The seagrass swayed in the wind

As if it too danced to the music

The sand shifted beneath his feet

As he crested the dune

Opening his view of the sea

Dark and monstrous

Spread out before him

The crescent moon, once lighting his path

Disappeared behind the clouds

Leaving him alone in the dark

Carefully, he descended

Listening to the sound of the surf

And the music calling him

Picking his way toward

The packed sand of the surf

When his footing changed,

He sighed a relief and picked a direction

Unsure where it would take him

Closer, further, he didn't know

His staff, stuck into the sand

A difficult and arduous task

The pull and sucking sound

Echoed in the night time as the staff

Slipped out of the harsh, packed sand

As his footsteps, sure and strong

Disappeared behind him

Washed away by the surf

Something called to him,

That pulled on his soul

The music, soft and lulling

Weaving him into a sense

Of complacency, of longing

For what, he didn't know

His steps, steadfast and strong

Kept pulling him forward

Footstep in front of footstep

Into the darkness

The moon slipped out

From behind the clouds

Lighting the scene in front of him

A boy, perched on a piano bench

Staring into the sea

His hands moving, his eyes unfocused

The notes intensified with each step

Something pulled at him

Ripping apart the fabric of his life

With each step, with each motion

Each note filling the air

Creating a pressure around him

A cocoon of music

Loud and brash echoing in his mind

He heard nothing beyond the notes

His thoughts disappeared

His everything centered

On the being in front of him

So caught up in the music

Lonely, haunting, and still

He stepped forward

Until he stood, perched on the sand

Next to this boy and his piano

He was transfixed, staring

Seeking a relief to the siren

That called him to this point

To this place and moment in time

The boy's gaze shifted

While his body remained as it was

Their eyes met, wise meeting wise

The man wasn't sure

Everything in him screamed to run

And yet, he stood still and frozen

Caught in this web of music

And the gaze of a young man

Who was wise beyond his years

The music continued to play

As the boy stood, climbing

He walked onto the piano

Perching until his gaze matched

Level-to-level

The boy reached out his hand

Staring in wonder, the man watched

As a golden light lifted, hovering

Above the boy's palm, rotating

Growing larger and stronger

Until it rose into the heavens

More and more stars rose

The man stood transfixed

Watching the creation of stars

And how they rose

Filling the night sky

His gaze followed the path

Of one as it slipped into the air

And nestled between the ones

That had come before it

Time disappeared, leaving them

Perched together watching

The night sky form

The man finally glanced down

Studying the boy in front of him

The music slowly faded

As the stars in his palms

Lifted into the sky

A moment of panic, the man felt

As he watched a final one form

The boy smiled up at him

Eager and kind

The moment the final star lifted

Leaving the boy's palm, he disappeared

The piano with him

Leaving the man alone, in the surf

Watching the final star

Make its place in the universe

Without the music, everything seemed dull

The man closed his eyes, reaching out

Hoping to hear the notes again

Pulling at him, calling to him

Loneliness filled him, leaving him shaken

He turned, glancing out at the sea

Now brilliantly sparkling with reflections

Of the twinkling stars in the night sky

Not a cloud, not the moon

Not even the sea expanded before him

Created a sense of awe like the stars

He sank to his knees, arms raised

Toward the majesty before him

Stars streaked across the sky, falling

His soul lit up, knowing that one day

The boy would be back

And the lull of those notes

Would call to his soul once again

Through

Through thick and thin you have been there

Every fallen tear, you and I share

When a talk needs to be had

You and I open even when it's bad

You and I share everything, our future our past

We try to make what we have last

You have brightened my life in every single way

Just for that I want to spend with you every day

We had some rough spots in our relationship

Not enough to make it completely rip

You have pushed me to be more

And helped me to find a few hidden doors

Whatever Shall Come

From the first look

That you gave me

And the first finger

I grasped

From the first minutes

I took a breath

And I became the one

To make my daddy

Look proud at the little

Bundle of joy he held

From the first small steps

And the first words I spoke

From these toddler years

To the small child

Who had no shyness

To the awkward teenager

Who graduated and grew

Thank you for sharing

The most precious years

Thank you for holding me

When I was in tears

Know I step into the world

Afraid and alone

Ready to face

Whatever shall come

Winter's Bite

The colors were brilliant

So brilliant show

Against the swirl

Of blue and white

All variants of red and oranges

And yellows collide

In an epic battle of supremacy

The nippy air stings

My nose with bitter regret

Of seasons gone by

So fleeting, the season

Of growth and sustenance

Dormancy is fast on your heels

Biting with wicked teeth

The shock of change is

Replaced with a sense of normalcy

Until once again

The balance shifts once again

Which Step

Relentless

Demanding

Pulling me limb

From bloody limb

I feel the ravages

Ripping the fibers

Of my muscles

Beneath sensitive skin

Too overwhelmed

By sensation

To find peace

And yet, I keep going

Each day

Forced to face

This new normal

Uncertain of the future

Ashamed of the past

Haunted and flayed

Alive among the present

I fear each step

Unsure and uncertain

Fearful of a life

Taken too early

An empty stomach

Stress upon stress

Heaped on each of us

Until we expire

Unable to swim

Through the thick

Jelly that has become

Our uncertain future

And still, I wake

I rise and take

One more step

Losing hope

Wishing for Release

As I walked further

Into the misty mount

The air, crispy and cool

Turns almost frigid and light

Moss conquers the floor

Trees lean and sway together

As the canopy blots out the sun

I cannot hear my footfall

Cushioned against the years

Of debris and renewal

The atmosphere is quiet

As if I am the interloper

Intruding upon nature

No bird song, no animal calls

Just me and my breath

A sense of peace overcomes me

As I scan the trees for predators

In the distance, I hear a roar

Not of a predator, but a crik

Instantly, I turn toward the sound

Moving with determination

I long to see the crystal clear

Breaking through the brush

I have the view I want

A fine mist of water

Teases my skin

Beneath the mid-day sun

I hear the splash of fish

And search fervently to locate them

Until my eyes find it

Beneath the clear water

My eyes follow their path

Shimmering, darting to and fro

And feel the serenity

That surrounds me

I close my eyes, listening

To the sounds of nature

In awe of the

Your Love

You have made my life so much better

You lift me up and showed me love

The love I have never been shown

You gave me the strength to carry on

With a life I would have rather not

And you handed me a gift so precious

You love me when I am down

You love me when it hurts

You love me no matter what

And you have given me

The best gift of all

Your love, your love, oh your love

You help me stand tall

Your hands hold me up

When I am feeling sad

They wipe away tears that fall

Your smile brightens my life

And your laughter cheers my soul

You love me when I am down

You love me when it hurts

You love me no matter what

And you have given me

The best gift of all

Your love, your love, oh your love

Your touch soothes my fears

The way you look at me

Puts me in tears

I have been a better person

For all that you do so thank you

Your support, your love,

And all that you do

You love me when I am down

You love me when it hurts

You love me no matter what

And you have given me

The best gift of all

Your love, your love, oh your love

Coming Soon

Into the Alaskan Wild – By Cristie Noll

Gwyn Branham is every bit the troubled woman people believe she is. Drug addicted. Party animal. Loner. She isn't surprised that no one came to save her after she has been kidnapped and hoisted away to the Alaskan wilderness. Locked in a cage, she is forced to go through drug withdrawal and left at the mercy of her captors who want nothing more than to possess and abuse her.

Lucas Thompson has loved Gwyn his entire life. She has been the breath in his lungs and the woman he envisioned for his future. Her flaws make her perfect. When she goes missing, he is a man bent on a mission – to save Gwyn and to shield her from the pain and abuse she suffered. He will do anything and everything to make sure she is alive and whole when she is freed.

Faced with challenges, can these two find each other? Or will the torture of it all tear them apart forever?

www.ingramcontent.com/pod-product-compliance
Lightning Source LLC
LaVergne TN
LVHW010109170826
845678LV00012B/2317

* 9 7 9 8 3 5 1 5 9 6 6 9 3 *